Colours We Eat

Brown Foods

Patricia Whitehouse

www.raintreepublishers.co.uk
Visit our website to find out more information about **Raintree** books.

To order:
Phone 44 (0) 1865 888112
Send a fax to 44 (0) 1865 314091
Visit the Raintree Bookshop at **www.raintreepublishers.co.uk** to browse our catalogue and order online.

First published in Great Britain by Raintree,
Halley Court, Jordan Hill, Oxford OX2 8EJ,
part of Harcourt Education.
Raintree is a registered trademark of Harcourt Education Ltd.

Editorial: Richard Woodham
Design: Richard Parker
Picture Research: Ruth Blair
Production: Kevin Blackman

Originated by Dot Gradations
Printed and bound in China by South China Printing Company

ISBN 1 844 21447 8
08 07 06 05 04
10 9 8 7 6 5 4 3 2 1

British Library Cataloguing in Publication Data
Whitehouse, Patricia
Brown Foods
641.3
A full catalogue record for this book is available from the British Library.

Acknowledgements
The publishers would like to thank the following for permission to reproduce photographs:
Heinemann Library pp. **5**, **7**, **8**, **10**, **14**, **15**, **16**, **17**, **18**, **19**, **20**, **21**, **22**, **24** (Que-Net); Corbis pp. **4** (Ed Young), **5**, **15R**, **13** (Charles O'Rear), **15L** (George D. Lepp); Getty Images p. **9L** (PhotoDisc); Masterfile p. **9R** (Kathleen Finlay); StockFood pp. **11** (Z. Sandmann/StockFood Munich), **12** (Brauner/StockFood Munich).

Cover photograph of chocolate drops reproduced with permission of Getty Images (Photodisc).

Every effort has been made to contact copyright holders of any material reproduced in this book. Any omissions will be rectified in subsequent printings if notice is given to the publishers.

CAUTION: Children should be supervised by an adult when handling food and kitchen utensils.

Some words are shown in bold, **like this.** You can find them in the glossary on page 23.

Contents

Have you eaten brown foods?

Colours are all around us.

How many different colours can you see in this picture?

All of these foods are brown.

Have you eaten any of them?

Which brown foods are big?

A turkey is big and brown.

People cook turkeys in an oven.

This **loaf** of brown bread is big.

Brown bread is good for you.

Which other brown foods are big?

Pancakes are made by cooking **batter** on a **griddle.**

The batter turns brown when it is cooked.

These pears are big and brown.

Pears grow on trees.

Which brown foods are small?

Some rice is brown.

People cook rice so it is soft enough to eat.

These olives are small and brown.

Olives grow on trees. They can also be green or black.

Which other brown foods are small?

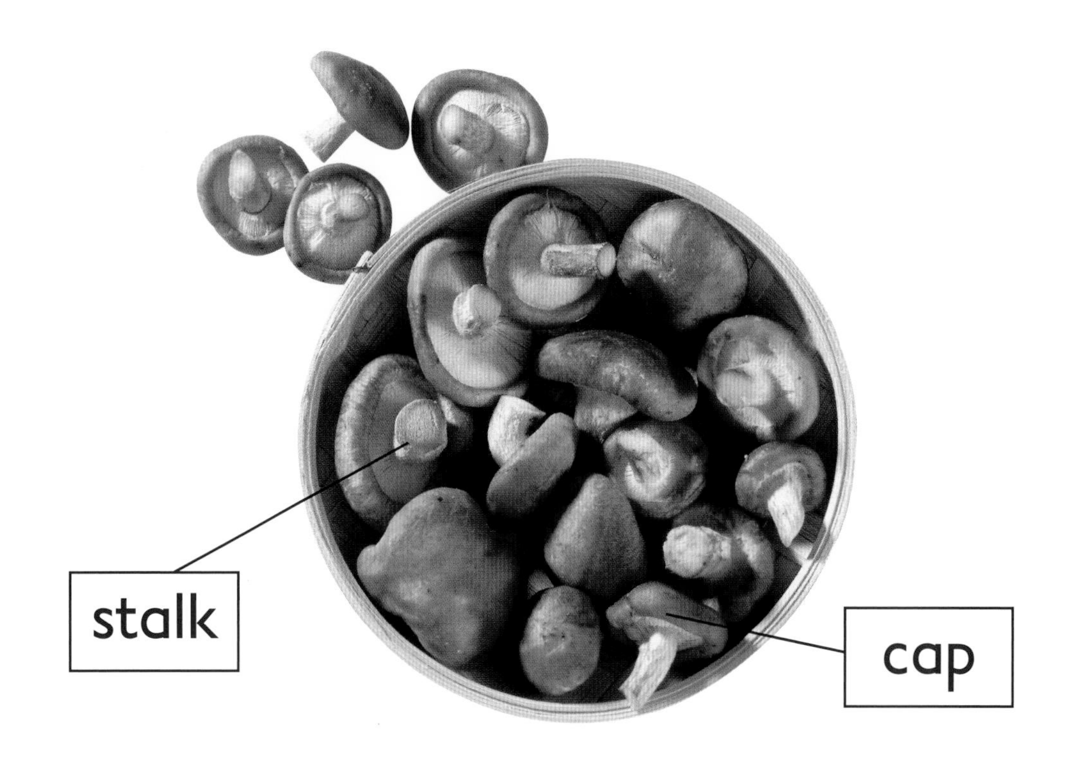

Some mushrooms are brown.

We usually eat the part called the cap.

Raisins are small and brown.

Raisins are dried green grapes.

Which brown foods are crunchy?

Pretzels are crunchy snacks.

They come in many different shapes.

Almonds are crunchy nuts.

They are the seeds of almond trees.

Which brown foods are soft?

peanuts

Peanut butter is soft.

It is made from chopped peanuts.

Some beans are brown.

Beans get soft when they are cooked.
These beans have been mashed.

Which liquids are brown?

You can drink hot chocolate.

It is made from **cocoa powder** and milk.

You can drink **miso soup**.

It is made by cooking **soybeans**.

Recipe: Peanut butter sandwich

Ask an adult to help you.

First, spread some peanut butter on brown bread.

Put another slice of bread on top.

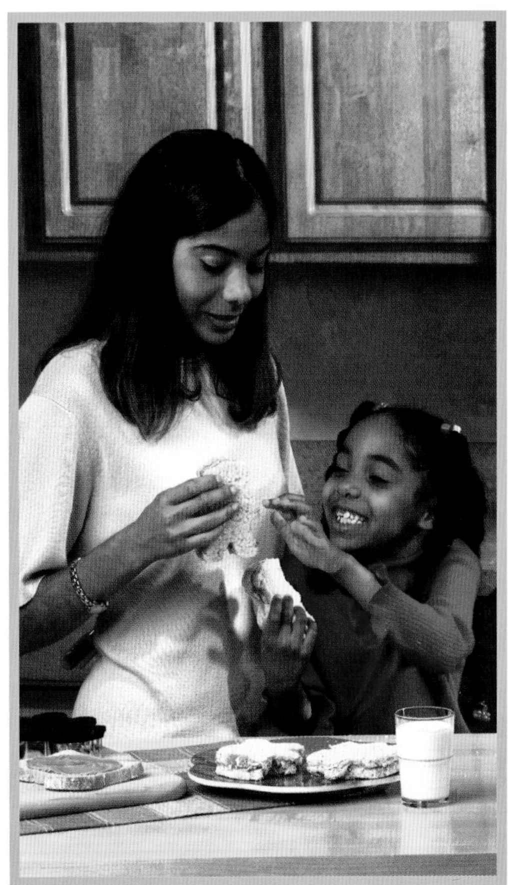

You could cut your sandwich into a bear shape with a **biscuit cutter.**

Then, eat your brown bear sandwich!

Quiz

Can you remember what these brown foods are called?

Look for the answers on page 24.

Glossary

batter
mixture of flour, eggs and milk used to make pancakes

biscuit cutter
used by cooks to cut food into shapes

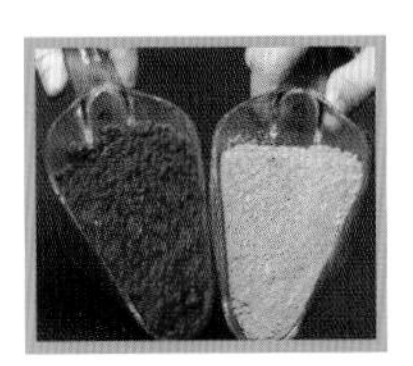

cocoa powder
makes hot chocolate when added to hot milk

griddle
hot iron plate used for cooking food

loaf
shaped lump of baked bread

miso soup
traditional Japanese soup

soybean
type of bean that grows on soya plants

Index

Answers to quiz on page 22

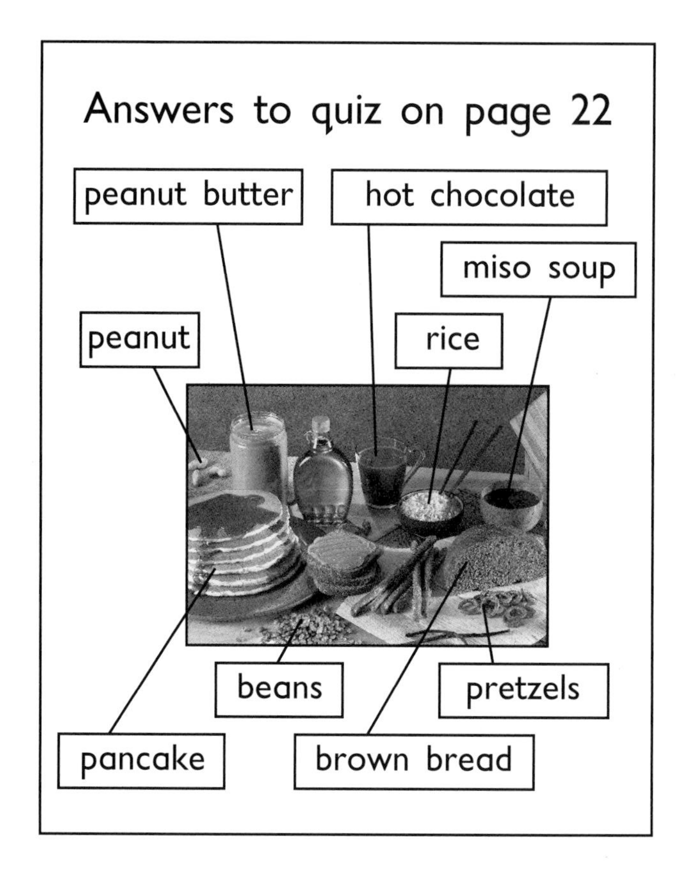

Titles in the Colours We Eat series include:

Hardback 184421446X

Hardback 1844214451

Hardback 1844214486

Hardback 1844214494

Hardback 1844214478

Find out about the other titles in this series on our website www.raintreepublishers.co.uk